WEIRD LOOKING ANIMALS ON LAND AND ON THE SEA

BABY PROFESSOR

EDUCATION KIDS

The strange, bizarre and just
plain weird looking creatures
of the animal kingdom.

The lowland
streaked tenrec
is found in
Madagascar.
If they are
threatened, they
will give warning
to their would
be assailant by
raising the spikes
surrounding
it's head and
stomping
their feet.

The komondor
is a large, white-
coloured dog
with a long,
corded coat.
The Komondor's
coat is long,
and thick, about
20 – 27 cm
long which
resembles
dreadlocks
or a mop.

Proboscis monkeys get their name because of their long noses. The word means 'nose'. They are known to make loud honking sounds with the help of their long noses.

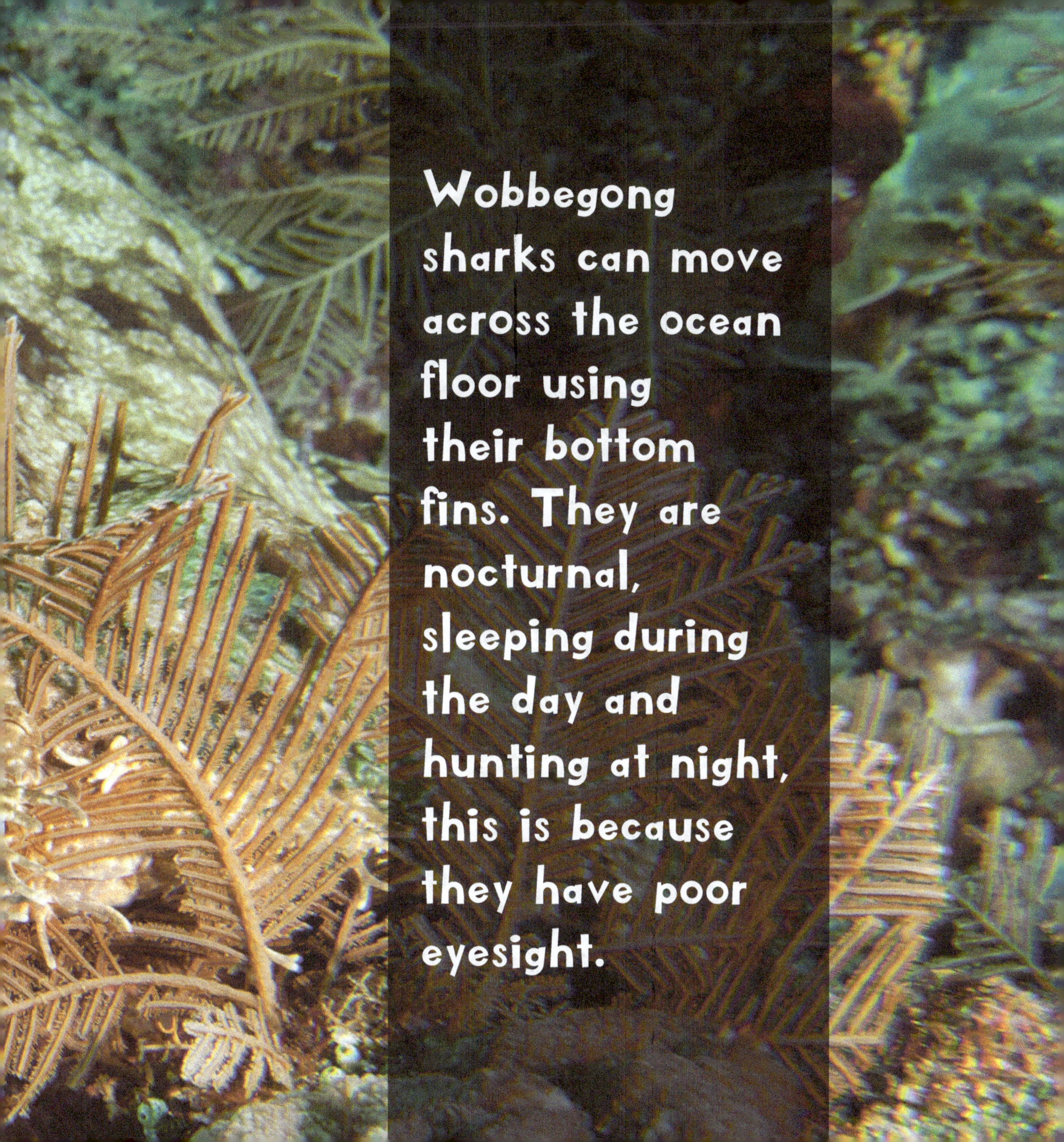

Wobbegong sharks can move across the ocean floor using their bottom fins. They are nocturnal, sleeping during the day and hunting at night, this is because they have poor eyesight.

The christmas tree worm is a colorful marine worm with beautiful, spiraling plumes that resemble a fir tree. They are commonly found embedded in entire heads of massive corals.

Leafy sea dragons are called by this name as they have what looks like a leaf on their body. Leafy sea dragons are carnivorous species, they primarily feed on tiny crustaceans and plankton.

The narwhal is the unicorn of the sea. Male narwhals possess a great spiraled tooth that projects from their heads. The ivory tusk tooth grows right through the narwhal's upper lip.